DEBT SUCKS!

*A College Student's Guide To Winning With Money
So They Can Live Their Dreams*

By: Ja'Net Adams

Dedication

I first want to say thank you to God who gave me this gift and also gives me the strength to share that gift with people around the world. Thank you to my husband Jon and my children Jonathan Jr. and Jocelyn who stood by my side as I wrote this book and always told me to keep going whenever I felt like slowing down! To my mother who taught me how to stand up for what I believe in and for being the person who told me to never use a credit card. Mom, you saved me thousands of dollars!

To my mother in law Patsy and father in law Ronald thank you for your continued love and support throughout the years. I truly appreciate everything you have done! Thank you to my brothers Barry, Chris, and James for always protecting me and being there for my family and I. To all of my friends who continually said, "I believe in you!", I thank you for the encouragement. Last, but not least to my mentor Morris your guidance truly has shorten my learning curve and has led me to a successful speaking career.

The Reason This Book Is Before You

I began writing this book over a year ago and I had written majority of the book, but for some reason I stopped writing and I put my pen down for months. On March 20, 2014 I received some horrible news that a young man by the name of Christopher Thomas had passed away. Christopher was someone that I had met a few years ago at a conference and we continued to cross paths from time to time in person and on social media. Christopher was an outstanding person who attended University of South Alabama and he was involved on campus in a variety of ways.

Every time I seen him in person he ALWAYS had a smile on his face and a upbeat attitude! Christopher had a bright future ahead of him and when I heard of his passing it truly sadden me. He was a supporter of this book and even submitted a question over social media that he wanted answered because he knew that it would help him and other college students with the same concern. Christopher is the reason that I picked my pen back up and didn't stop writing until the book was finished. It is students like him that keep me going because I want to help every student that I can live their dreams! Christopher you are deeply missed and I am thankful for the time we were able to spend together!

Table of Contents

CHAPTER ONE
The Day That Changed My Life!

Almost every college has required reading for incoming freshmen. I don't know why they have it, maybe they want to make sure you can read before you set foot on campus or they can't stand the thought of you having a three month break from thirteen years of reading before going into four more years of reading! I attended South Carolina State University and the summer before my freshman year I, and every other incoming freshman was asked to read three books before we arrived for freshman orientation in August. I read all three over the summer and was ready to answer any questions about the books at freshman orientation. Each day during the week long orientation I waited patiently for one of the student leaders to ask a question about what was in those books. I was ready to share with them my immense knowledge about the books, and guess what? *Not one question was asked!*

During freshman year and the two years that followed it looked like I had completely wasted my time the summer after high school graduation. By junior year of college I could only remember the name of one of the books that I had read that summer. The reason that I remembered what the book was about was because it was based on true events that had happened at the university. The book was called the "Orangeburg Massacre" by Jack Nelson and Jack Bass. The Orangeburg Massacre was an event that occurred in 1968 during the civil rights movement in Orangeburg, SC. There was a bowling alley in Orangeburg that would not allow African Americans to enter its doors because of segregation. It was the only bowling alley near the historically Black college and university so if African American students were banned from it, then they had nowhere to bowl.

The actual event took place on February 8, 1968 when 200 people, the majority of which were students were on campus decided to protest against the segregation at the bowling alley. Police arrived and tensions escalated to the point that police started shooting into the crowd. Twenty eight people were injured and three students were killed. Samuel Hammond Jr. and Henry Smith were students at South Carolina State University while the third victim, Delano Middleton was still in high school. This tragic event happened on the land that I now walked on as a student so you can see how I could never forget the book.

I was a marketing major at South Carolina State which meant that I spent almost every waking moment at the Belcher Hall School of Business. I had different classes and different meetings at different times, every week while in college. Sometimes I didn't know whether I was coming or going, but there was one day out of the week that I knew where I was going to be at a certain time all four years of college and that was Wednesday. Every Wednesday at noon all business school students were required to be in the fourth floor auditorium for the Executive Speaker Series. The Executive Speaker Series was where the Business School would invite CEO's and top executives from all around the country to come speak to the business students about Corporate America and different business concepts that propelled their careers to new heights. I actually enjoyed going to the Executive Speaker Series each week. I loved hearing different business leaders speak about their experiences and what it takes to be the best! From freshman to junior year I always rushed to the auditorium so that I could sit in one of the seats in the first five rows. Didn't matter which seat as long as it was in one of those first five! You could say that for roughly 114 Wednesday's my routine stayed the same until one Wednesday my junior year.

One Wednesday I did not rush to the Executive Speaker Series. That morning I think I had received a bad grade on an exam and was given one of my many parking tickets. Both situations put me in a 'who cares' type of mood. I remember stepping into the fourth floor auditorium with my best friend Eboni and instead of dragging her to the front seats, I turned to her and said "I'm not feeling this today, so let's just sit back here in the back, so whoever they have speaking today as soon as they get done we can leave and go to the cafe!" Eboni agreed so we sat down and not only did I sit in the back, but I sat as close to the wall as I could so I could have somewhere to put my arm up against and put my head in my hand. This Wednesday, "The Wednesday", something was different. The dean of the business school had invited someone different to come speak to us. The speaker still was a top executive at a top Fortune 100 company, but he also was an alum of South Carolina State. His name was Hank Allan and he was a Regional Director at Pfizer Pharmaceuticals. Instead of him going into how great he was as a businessman he started asking questions about the Orangeburg Massacre, and not just asking questions, but for every correct answer he was giving the student a crisp fifty dollar bill! Before the money came out I looked like I wanted to be anywhere else besides that auditorium, but all of a sudden I was sitting straight up in my chair with a smile on my face trying to get Hank's attention! In my head I was saying to myself "this is the day that you have been waiting for! Ja'Net, you read the "Orangeburg Massacre" three years ago and now it is about to pay off!" He asked the first question, my hand goes up. This girl in the front row on the left side got the fifty dollars. He asked the second question. My hand shoots up again! A guy in the third row on the right side, received the fifty dollars. He asked questions three and four, two people in the center, second and fourth row they received the fifty dollars. Fifth question, sixth question! By this time I had decided to keep my hand in the air, waving it frantically trying to get Hank's attention. I was trying so hard I almost pushed Eboni out of her chair onto the floor, but it didn't matter because Hank could not see me!

The day had finally come for me to be rewarded for my hard work of reading that book and I missed it. On that Wednesday, "The Wednesday" I let my guard down. On "The Wednesday" I decided not to do my best and it cost me $300! I don't know what day it is that you are reading this book, but whatever day it is, it is your "The Wednesday!" It is your "The Wednesday" when it comes to your finances and today you decide on whether you are going to keep your guard up or are you going to let it down. Those who decide to do their best are the ones who win at money. First you have to determine within you, what's your motivation.

CHAPTER TWO
What's Your Motivation?

Dreams are motivators, because dreams are what you are passionate about. You cannot achieve anything in life if you don't feel that something better is coming your way. This is especially true when it comes to getting out of debt. It doesn't matter if the debt is small or large you have to be motivated to pay it off. Take a moment right now and think about what your dreams are for your life. If you are having difficulty deciding what your dreams are, think about what you would do in your life if money was not an issue. Now that you have your dreams in your head it is time to get those dreams out of your head and down onto paper. This piece of paper will be known as your "Dream Sheet." The reason that the dreams have to be written out is because that way the dreams are real now and it forces you to make them become reality.

Once your dreams hit the "Dream Sheet" they are now goals that you are striving to achieve and the easiest way to achieve goals is to give each one a deadline. The timeframe of your goals should be separated into short, intermediate, and long term goals. Short term goals are those goals that you want to achieve in six months or less. For example maybe your goal for spring semester is to get a paid internship for the summer or the fall semester. If you achieve this short term goal of landing a paid internship it will lead to a paycheck that you can use to pay off debt.

Intermediate goals are the goals that you want to have completed one to two years from now. These dreams take a little more time and work to achieve so they are put in the intermediate section. For example an intermediate goal for a sophomore in college maybe to make sure that in exactly two years that they will be walking across the stage receiving their diploma. There are a lot of students who do not graduate in four years and that costs them money. For the fifth year of college the individual takes on more debt and misses out on a year that they could have been making a salary.

Long term goals are those goals that will take you three to five years to complete. Long term goals are intense and take many more action steps to achieve. You have to be careful with long term goals because it is easy to lose focus on them while you are trying to accomplish the short and intermediate goals. Think of a junior in college who decides that in five years they would like to be in their second year of working as a corporate attorney at a Fortune 500 company. This is a very specific five year dream that the junior will have to stay focus on so that all the necessary action steps (graduate, pass the LSAT, Law School, pass the bar exam, interview and get hired by a Fortune 500 company) are carried out.

A simple way to accomplish your short, intermediate, and long term goals is to have some of them relate to each other. Make a short term goal relate to a long term goal so that when you achieve the short term goal it is actually pushing toward completing the long term goal quicker! When I was a freshman in college I had a long term goal of having an internship leading into my senior year. I did not have a company in mind, but I did know wherever I did the internship I wanted it to be the company I worked for after graduation. In order to make this dream a reality I needed to put some short and intermediate goals in place. Short term goals as a freshman were first and foremost to get good grades that first semester. Also I looked into the career center on campus to see what the internship possibilities were at the time so I would know what companies offered students and at what time of the year. The intermediate goals were based solely on timing. See I was in college on a tennis scholarship, and tennis unlike other sports is year round so I had tennis matches in the fall and spring semester.

I decided that I could only do internships in the fall of senior year because there was usually only one tournament that happened in the fall semester. It was a warm-up tournament for the spring semester. Also if I was going to do an internship in the fall of senior year I needed to be ahead in my college credits so that I could miss that semester and still graduate on time. Short and long term goals were set, but it was the intermediate goals that would help me accomplish the long term goal. The summers after my freshman and sophomore year I took summer classes at a local college in my hometown. This helped me get a year ahead in my credits. My other intermediate goal was to get involved on campus so that I would have something other than tennis on my resume. I joined the National Business Fraternity Alpha Kappa Psi as well as another business organization within the business school. The combination of the short term goal of a great GPA and the intermediate goals of accelerated credits and campus involvement helped me achieve my long term goal of a paid internship! This was not just some minor internship, but this company paid me an annual salary of $45,000! Which meant I was bringing home $3,000 a month! Not only were they paying me, but they also paid for me to have a two bedroom apartment in downtown Minneapolis, Minnesota where the internship was located. They also provided me with a car and free gas for the entire length of the eight month internship so all I had to pay for was my food! Without having my goals in place I would have never had a chance at the internship.

You may be thinking to yourself "why do I have to think of goals and write them down?" The reason is because your goals are dreams, and if you don't have dreams that you want to come true in the future, there is no way you will make it a priority to control your money! So if you are serious about getting out of whatever debt your are in and moving toward a future where your dreams are pushed out of your head and into the real world, then you need to write them down and put the sheet in a place where you can see it every morning. Now that you have your motivation staring back at you every morning it is now time to get your money under control!

CHAPTER THREE
Where Did It Go?

I am the poster child of the phrase "where did it go?" I actually attended college on a tennis scholarship which means that for four years my classes were free, my books were free, my food was free, and everything that had to do with college was free! In fact thanks to the tennis scholarship and the eight month internship I did, I graduated from college debt free with $10,000 in my bank account! I can imagine the look of disbelief on your face right now. Disbelief because you are reading a book that I wrote that is supposed to be about how to get out of debt. Someone who graduated with no debt and $10K in the bank should not have any problems starting their life after college and I didn't at first, but then life started to happen.

I was living in Bloomington, Indiana working for this company while my high school sweetheart was living an eight hour drive away in North Carolina. He didn't stay my boyfriend long because a couple of years after graduation we got married. Once we were married I found out that he had $25,000 in student loans for one year of college! I was in complete shock when I found this out because the entire time we were in college I thought he was on a basketball scholarship all four years, but in reality the college basketball coach convinced his parents to send him to a private college and pay for the first year themselves. That plan would have been fine at a $7,000 a year college or maybe even an $11,000 a year institution, this college was $25,000 *for one year*!

To put this number into perspective my husband could have gone to South Carolina State University as an out of state student for all four years and only paid $28,000 total. We were already married when I found out about this debt so there was no turning back. I remember telling him that the student loans belonged to him and "his" paycheck was going to pay for them, because I had bigger plans for "my" money and it didn't involve paying off someone else's student loans. We had been married for about a month so the next logical step obviously was to build a house!

Not just any kind of house, but we built a house that was bigger than both of our parents homes. I as well as you, are part of the microwave generation. The microwave generation means exactly what it sounds like. Whenever you want quick food at home, you throw it in the microwave and three minutes later you have a meal in front of you. That is how we live our lives, because we have to have everything right now. Waiting is NOT an option! That is the only explanation that makes sense for why Jon and I would trade a $700 a month two bedroom, two bathroom apartment with all utilities paid for a $1500 a month mortgage where we pay for the lights, AND the gas, AND the water, AND the repairs, AND the trash, AND, AND, AND! Impatience rules the microwave generation and because of it we make decisions that put us in debt for years. I didn't care what we had to do, I wanted my dream home built! Never mind that we already had $25,000 of debt attached to us. *Who cares!* I thought, because it was "his" debt and not "mine" that it was okay if I add a "no money down" $230,000 mortgage on top of it! In my head

I rationalized this decision by saying we make enough money to afford the house.

Well we moved into the house and after about a year my husband's car, that he'd had since college, started needing repairs. I am so smart, I mean I graduated Summa Cum Laude so my bright idea of let's trade the car in was obviously the best decision. So I thought. Not only did we trade it in, but we purchased a brand new all white Chrysler 300 for $23,000! Once again I found myself having a heart to heart with my husband as we were leaving the car dealership. I looked at him and said "you know this is your car, which means your paycheck is going to pay for it!" Clearly I had not grasped the fact of what the preacher said on our wedding day when he said "and now you are one," because that also meant our debt.

Before we go any further let's do a quick recap. I graduated from college debt free with $10,000 and within a few years I was more than $48,000 in debt! I would love to tell you that on my own I decided enough was enough, but that would be a lie. Life decided for me because one fall day life slapped me in the face with a brick and I was laid off from my job. All of a sudden the walls came crashing down, reality was starting to set in and I realized that I was $48,000 in debt not including our house and there was no way to pay for it! That's when I woke up! That's when I realized that for the last few years I thought I was controlling my money, but it was controlling me! I thought we were moving forward in life with the new jobs, new house, and new car, but in reality we were moving backwards and we were moving backwards fast! Jon and I were on a clear path to lose it all and to make the situation even scarier we had a one year old son at home depending on us.

I decided to ask myself right then "Where did it all go? Where did the money I made over the last few years go? How did I get into all of this debt? How am I going to get out of it?" These are the questions that I asked myself before I started on my two and a half year journey to become debt free.

How many times do you find yourself saying "where did all my money go?" How many times have you started your day off with a twenty dollar bill in your pocket and by the end of the day you only had coins left? If you find that your money goes as quickly as it comes then you do not have control over your money. In fact your money has control over you. When you figure out where the money you have goes every month that is the time when you can start to find the extra money to pay off debt (student loans, credit cards, car loans, etc).

The easiest way to find out what you are spending your money on is to track it. For two weeks preferably at the beginning of the month track everything that you are spending your money on. Do you have a cell phone bill that you pay for? Do you live in an apartment off campus where you have to pay rent and utilities? These are expenses that have to be included. EVERYTHING that takes money out of your pocket is an expense even if it is something as small as a pack of gum that you bought from the gas station. It counts! For the two weeks save any receipts that you get from purchases so that you can keep up with the money spent. Once the two weeks are up it is time to write all the expenses down in one place.

Everything is easier to control when it is written out on paper. Now that you have spent two weeks finding out how much money you spend on a monthly basis it is time to create your own personal "spending plan." Why call it a "spending plan" and not a "budget?" The reason that it is called a "spending plan" is because there is so much fear in the word "budget" that people dismiss it as soon as they hear the word. Some think that budgets are made to put handcuffs on them and to ruin their lives. Budgets actually take the handcuffs off, but to make it easier we will stick with calling it a "spending plan." The spending plan will be in column form where on the left side you will have income written on the first line and to the right of the paper you are to write your income. Your income can be money you get from a work study or a part time job. Income can even be money you get from your parents every month. Once you write down your income, go down a few spaces below

Income write out the word "Expenses." Under it start listing every expense you have tracked the past two weeks. If you have six expenses all six of those expenses need to go under the expense column one after the other. Then whatever the amount that you spent on that expense that number goes to the right. For example if you spend sixty dollars a month on your cell phone bill then "cell phone" goes in the left column under expense and sixty dollars goes to the right.

When your spending plan is done then you need to figure out how much debt you are in. As a professional speaker who speaks on college campuses all over the United States, I have found that students are in many types of debt, not just student loans. Students are in credit card debt, medical debt, car loan debt, and more, in addition to having student loans. In order to find out how much student loan debt you're in, you many need to call your parents or the company that services your loan to find out the exact amount. You have to know the amount of debt you're in so that you can start to find the money to pay it off in the future. It is make it or break it time now, because it is in the next step that I see a lot of people give up because they don't want to truly be debt free. They actually like living in the present spending money when they want. The ones that stick it out from here on out are the ones who live debt free and are able to live their dreams! Which person will you be? Let's find out.

CHAPTER FOUR
Cut It Out!

Once I figured out that we were $48,000 in debt my husband and I sat down and put our spending plan together. This actually was the easy part and it was the next phase that was the hard work. It was time for us to start cutting some things out of the spending plan. Everything that wasn't necessary had to go! Even some necessary items had to be cut back. We went through every line item on the spending plan and figured out how we could adjust it to save money. Magazine and newspaper subscriptions cut out! We called the cable company and reduced the channels so that we could have a lower monthly bill.

We called the cell phone companies and reduced our minutes and data plans so that bill could be reduced. We stopped eating out and focused on getting enough food at the grocery store each month so we would not be tempted to go to a restaurant and spend money. As for the groceries we adjusted what we bought. We stopped buying steaks and brand name foods. We stuck to the less expensive meats like pork chops and chicken. If there was a generic or store brand for the food item we bought it. No more cereal that had a captain or a leprechaun on it in our household. We didn't go on any vacations for two and a half years, and we didn't buy anyone birthday or Christmas gifts either including each other! We didn't buy clothes or shoes the entire time except for our growing child. We wanted to make sure every dollar went to paying off the debt.

We looked into how much we were spending on our electric, water, and gas bills and came up with ways to reduce them. We made sure every light was turned off and everything was unplugged with the exception of the refrigerator. When we washed clothes we made sure to wash with cold water because that reduced our gas bill. If it was sixty to seventy degrees outside we would turn off our heating/air-condition unit and that would lower the energy bill for the month. Sometimes we were able to go days without turning the heat or air-condition on. These are just a few examples of how we were able to cut back to find money to pay off our debt.

As a college student you shouldn't have as many expenses as we had, but I am sure there are some expenses you have that could be cut back. Let's start with the cell phone which almost every college student has in their possession. You should look at your monthly bill and see how many minutes you are using and the data plan you have. Then go to the cell phone carrier's store or call their customer service department and reduce your plan down to a lower price. The best option is to get a monthly prepaid plan because they are cheap and can save you a lot of money. If you are on a meal plan make sure to use it. It makes no sense to skip meals that are paid for so you can go out and spend money at a restaurant.

Do you have any memberships that you are paying for such as organizations on campus? Organizations tend to have yearly dues involved with them, so if you are in a tight spot financially the organization that you are involved in may need to take a back seat for the time being.

For those of you who live off campus there are a few ways to save money. Students who stay off campus usually don't have meal plans, but instead buy groceries and cook, so their grocery bill is where they are going to save money. If you have a roommate and share the groceries then that roommate needs to be on board with saving money. If they are not on board then you need to only buy food for yourself so you can control your spending. To start saving on groceries you need to have the grocery store's reward card because each week grocery stores have sales that are only available to those customers with a rewards card. For example the store may offer buy two packs of bacon, approximately seven dollars each and get three packs of bacon free. You pay fourteen dollars for thirty-five dollars worth of bacon and end up saving twenty-one dollars! The true deal is that bacon will last the entire semester, especially if you freeze it until you are ready to cook it. Grocery stores are also a great place to use coupons. Before you start to frown about the thought of using a coupon, hear me out. Coupons can make a $100 grocery bill turn into a thirty dollar grocery bill. You don't have to be extreme with coupons and start hoarding food, but you can get a few coupons a month to lower your grocery bill. Coupons are not just for groceries, but coupons are offered for almost everything. There are discount coupons for restaurants, movie theaters, yoga, haircuts, vacations, massages, etc, so you can save money in any activity you do!

As a college student you are actually a walking discount yourself. There are plenty of businesses that give college student discounts as long as you are able to show your id. The supermarket, movie theaters, museums, cell phone companies, clothing retailers, restaurants, and computer companies have offered college students discounts over the years. You have to put it in your mind that your motto is going to be "I will not pay full price for anything!" Instead of paying nine plus dollars to go see a movie, wait for the movie to come out on Redbox for a dollar. No need for you to pay for cable if you live off campus. Cable and internet can easily cost $120 or more a month, but if you cut out the cable and get an eight dollar membership to Hulu or Netflix, you have lowered your expense by eighty dollars, because that's how much the cable portion usually costs. What about the text books that you need every semester? Ask every professor if the textbook is a necessity for the class and if not that is money that you can save. You can try to share textbooks with another person. I had a friend who was not the same major as I was, but because she was a business major overall we had some of the same core classes. As a scholarship athlete I was able to get all of my books for free and that allowed her the opportunity not to buy some of her textbooks and share with me instead, saving her hundreds of dollars.

Another money drainer for college students are cars and everything that comes with having a car. When anyone gets a car there is so much more cost to having it than a car payment. There is the cost of gas that has to go into it every week. There is also the monthly car insurance that has to be paid and depending on the year of the car will determine how high the payment will be. Newer model cars cost much more in car insurance payments. Don't forget about the maintenance of the car, because at some point it will cost you some money. You will have to pay to get the oil changed, car inspection, license tags, windshield wipers, tires rotated, property taxes, and more. This is just to keep it in good shape. Most individuals get into debt because of cars breaking down. The person will have little to no savings and need something like new brakes and because they can't pay cash for the brakes they have to use a credit card.

If you don't have a car now and live on campus there is no need to go into debt to have one because every place you need to get to is where you live at. What if you live off campus and don't have a car? You still have the option of public transportation whether it is riding the bus or the subway. For those who live off campus and already have a car you can save money by carpooling with others. This way everyone saves money.

The point of all of this is to cut back as much as you can so that you can have breathing room. Once you have done that then it is time to flip the switch!

CHAPTER FIVE
Sell, Sell, SELL!

I am the queen of selling anything! I have been making money since I was a little girl. I became an entrepreneur in the second grade and my first product came in a Ziplock bag. Every night you could find me in my mother's kitchen mixing Koolaid and sugar together and packaging it in Ziplock bags. I would take the Ziplock bags to school every day and sell them at lunch for twenty-five cents a bag. I would spend my morning on the bus and in class promoting my product so everyone would spread the word about my sugary goodness! By the time lunch rolled around the kids were lined up to buy from me. I was selling out every day, I was really on my way to a running a million dollar empire off of Koolaid packets and sugar! That was until the "man" aka the principal shut my operations down and told me to move my business outside of school walls.

My next business was outside of school walls, in fact it was inside my house. My parents gave me a bubble gum machine for Christmas when I was in the fifth grade. It was sky blue and you could put small bubble gum balls inside of it. There was a slot where you put money inside, but you didn't have to in order to get the gum. You could just turn the knob and the gum would come out. The coin slot was really just for show until I decided to use it to make money off the neighborhood kids. One thing that I know about kids is that they love sugar and that love got me twenty-five cents per piece of gum. Kids would come ring my doorbell and I would answer the door holding my sky blue bubblegum machine. This business was raking in the money! I was getting an average of a dollar per kid.

During middle school and high school I worked for other people teaching tennis for ten dollars an hour. It wasn't until I got to college that I truly started making money. I went to college three hours away from home, so my mother worried about me being that far away so she made sure that I had everything that she thought I needed.

She made me a personalized first aid kit that had some items in it, that if I did get hurt I would know how to use them to tend to my injury. She also made sure I had drinks and snacks in case there was ever a time the cafeteria was closed and I became hungry, I would not starve to death. There was one snack that I would never eat and throughout the entire first semester of freshman year it would just sit there. Until one day my roommate asked me "since you are not going to eat those, can I have one?" The snack that she was asking about were my chips. It was the box of variety chips that came twenty to a box and my mother would bring me two boxes a semester. When my roommate asked me that question an idea automatically popped into my head. I asked myself, "Why am I letting these chips go to waste, instead of selling them?" I gave my roommate that first bag of chips for free because she gave me the idea, but after that everyone paid a dollar per bag! My best customers were my roommates, tennis teammates and even some of the football team. The only thing they had to say around me was "I am so hungry and the cafeteria doesn't open for another hour! I don't want to waste gas to go off campus to pay for food!" That's when Ja'Net their hero would come to their rescue with a bag of chips for a dollar. In my past money making ventures other than the principal in elementary school I have never had anyone try to keep me from selling items for money until I started selling these chips!

My roommate who gave me the idea to sell the chips was the main one trying to run my customers away! She would say in front of my best customers, "Ja'Net! How are you going to sell us something that your mother gives you for free?" I would look at her with a smile on my face and say, "Are you hungry, or are you not?" That usually resulted in her first giving me my dollar and then snatching the chips out of my hands! Selling chips was just the beginning!

Throughout college I made money typing papers for students as well as tutoring students who were weak in a certain class and needed help to bring their grade up in that class. I would sell "stuff" out of my dorm room. Every now and then I would look around my dorm room or my room at home and see "stuff" I didn't want any more or didn't use and I would look for people on campus to sell it to.

In college any of the money I was making was for me to have spending money every month since I was on scholarship that's all I needed it for at the time. Learning how to make money by selling anything really helped me out when I found myself in $48,000 of debt and no job. After we found all the extra money we could in the spending plan by cutting everything we could out, it was then time to sell everything we didn't use or did not need! I started looking for big "stuff" to sell first. I looked around our house and we had FIVE TV's in a house that only consisted of two and a half people (the half being my one year old). I thought to myself why are the TV's outnumbering the people in this house, so I took three of the TV's to different pawn shops and sold them. Then I looked for other electronics and found VCR's, DVD players, stereos, and took those to the pawn shop. I even found a microwave that someone gave us as a wedding present sitting in a closet! Of course it was sold too! Next category of "stuff" to sell was jewelry, particularly gold jewelry. Jewelry stores and pawn shops buy gold, but jewelry shops give you the best value. I looked through the house and found any gold jewelry broken or not and took it to the local jewelry shop. A small handful of jewelry got me $200 plus dollars. After seeing how much money I could get from selling gold I started asking friends and family if they had any broken gold and if they did I offered to do the work to get them the best price in exchange for a ten percent fee.

After the bigger and pricier items were sold for money, it was close to summer which is prime yard sale time so I started gathering up all that I could for multiple yard sales over the summer. People buy anything at a yard sale so I looked at everything as having a value to someone. I started with wedding presents that we weren't using then I went into my closet and Jon went into his and we took out all the clothes that we no longer wore. We gathered up shoes, clocks, old cell phones, toys, purses, paintings, college textbooks, *anything*, and we set it up outside our home on Saturdays and sold it! We sold the items at a premium price too! There was no way that someone was going to buy an unopened brand name blender for fifty cents! They paid fifteen dollars and if they didn't want it because of the price, I knew the next person would. You always have to keep in mind that the reason that you did all the work to have a yard sale was to make money so that you can pay off debt, so don't let anyone cheat you out of that! All the money we made selling anything went to paying off debt. We did not use it to go on vacation or buy new furniture it was all done so we could get closer to being debt free.

What do you have that you could sell? Look around your dorm for "stuff" you don't need, when you are at home during a school break look there too. Also ask your parents or guardians if there is anything that they don't want anymore and then ask can you have it. If you decided to cut off cable and only watch your favorite TV shows and movies on a computer then you can sell your TV for extra money. You can have your own yard sale on campus or even out of your room. Print up flyers and pass them out during the week of the sale. There are students who will buy from you especially if you are selling a textbook from a class that you took last semester that they are now taking. I know you will get more money out of that student than you would selling the book back to the bookstore.

Also if you have a private owned bookstore around campus or near where you live at home you could take any type of book, textbook or not to that store and sell them. These type stores usually will also buy CDs from you as well so they can sell them in their store. You have the option of eBay or other resale sites that may provide you with more money for your stuff than a yard sale would. If you sell on a site like eBay your stuff needs to be more updated. For example if for your birthday or Christmas you received a sweater from your aunt and you don't like it, there may be someone in Indiana who absolutely loves it and will pay money for it! This sale is all profit for you because someone else spent their money and gave it to you. Selling your blood is another option that students do to make money. Students go to sell their blood multiple times during each semester because it is easy money.

Once you sell everything you can it is time to look at yourself. What talents or skills do you have that you can make money doing? You may be saying to yourself "I don't have any skills that other people would pay for." You would be surprised at what you have to offer if you truly think about it. Did you play a sport growing up? Even if you are not in college on an athletic scholarship I am sure you know enough of that sport to teach it to a kid in elementary school that is just starting off in that sport. There are parents that are willing to pay you ten dollars an hour to help their child excel to be a better athlete. Do you play an instrument? Why not teach children how to play that instrument. The guitar, piano, or drum are all great instruments to make money with teaching.

Were you always the one your friends would come see to get their hair done? You can set up your own beauty parlor or barbershop in your dorm room or apartment and charge for your services. The clients will come because you are less expensive than the professionals. In college I knew a young lady who could braid hair and she would braid several women's heads a week for eighty dollars each! That is at least $320 a week while going to school full time! She always had customers because to get your hair braided professionally costs $200 so she was undercutting the professionals and therefore winning the business! Is there one school subject that you excel at? I am sure there are high school students and even some people on campus who would love for you to share your expertise. One of my tennis teammates was a genius at math and would tutor others for money and since she was on academic scholarship any money she made she was able to save! Are there any hard classes in your major that you already passed with an A or B? Offer the students currently in the class help if they are struggling, because you already know the material and can guide the student to pass the class!

I don't want to leave out those of you who are artsy, because I think you have a larger audience you can reach. For those of you who paint you can sell your paintings in more places than just on campus. There are restaurants and other businesses such as hair salons that display artwork from a different artist each month and they will let you put a price on them so that the paintings can be sold. You can also sell your artwork online where the world is your customer. If you are someone who makes jewelry or unique pieces of clothing you can also sell on the Internet through various websites. You also have a great customer base right on campus because students want original pieces that no one else has!

These are just a few examples of how you can look at what you like to do for free and turn it into a business that can make you some extra money! When you figure it out and start making money you then need to figure out what to do with that money. The answer may seem obvious, but you would be surprised how many people whether they are in college or not get it wrong!

CHAPTER SIX
Save, For What?

Plenty of students are creative when it comes to making money. Innovative ideas flow freely when making money comes into play. Where students run into trouble is deciding what to do with the money they make. The most common use for extra money in the past has been to spend it as soon as it touches your hand, but there is a much better way, and this way leads to long term financial success. A better option for newly acquired money is to save it!

When people hear this advice a frown usually appears on their face because saving is not fun. Spending is! With saving you are not supposed to touch the money and it just sits there while everything you think you want at the mall comes and goes! Saving takes discipline and hard work and that is why so many fail at it! You have to realize that you're not saving money just to be saving money, you're saving money because you are breathing!

Yes, because you are breathing you have to save money. At all times you need to have an emergency fund or what I like to call an "if you are breathing fund!" I call it that because if you are breathing something can happen and that will cause you to have to spend money! And whatever that "something" is, you don't want to have a zero balance in your emergency fund because that leads to you borrowing money and in turn putting you into deeper debt! If you have money set aside for an unforeseen event, that event can take place and it will not put you into a financial tailspin! One of the major factors of students dropping out a college is financial distress. A student can have a $500 emergency and because they can't find a way to get the money they have to drop out of college in order to get a job to pay it back. Students run into various money emergencies throughout their time in college.

When I started to write this book students reached out to me and shared some common and uncommon emergencies that they ran into. A common emergency at the beginning of each semester is students not having enough money for all their books, leaving them to have to borrow from others, or go without the needed book all semester. One student shared with me that one semester he was playing intramural sports, injured his leg and went to the emergency room. The real emergency was not his leg, but the medical bill that came later which amounted to hundreds of dollars because he didn't have health insurance. Another common emergency that a student shared with me was that "if you are breathing" and have a car you are going to have car problems. Car problems can range from a minor tail light out, which costs about $100 to a major situation like the need for engine repair, costing about $3,000 and depending on the problem, a student who needs their car to get to their job could end up losing out on hours of work and many even lose their job, because they don't have transportation for a few days!

Financial aid is another issue that can cause students distress at the beginning of a semester. If there is a delay in receiving financial aid a student could be at risk and not be able to register for classes. There are instances at higher education institutions where they will put "pending financial aid" on your paperwork so that you can register for your classes. If the financial aid does not come through the student has to pay the balance or drop some classes. I met a student at one of the schools that I was speaking at, where this had taken place during freshman orientation. The student was one of the upperclassman responsible for a group of the incoming freshman. She pulled me aside and told me that a portion of her financial aid that she had last school year was not going to be available to her this school year. The amount missing totaled $1000 and there was no way she was going to be able to come up with the money because her parents didn't have it and neither did she. She said, if she didn't find the money in a week she would have to drop classes which she cannot afford to do because it would delay her graduation date in the future.

These are just a few examples and I am sure you can think of a few times in your life where you wish there was extra money saved! Now from this day forward you can start saving and building up that "if you're breathing fund!"

We've already discussed how you can make money off of your hobbies and talents then save the money you make, but how else can you get some money? I remember walking around campus second semester of my freshman year and I was seeing students with brand new clothes, some wearing a new pair shoes every day, and even some driving new cars. I remember going to my friend's dorm room and seeing her new forty inch flat screen TV!

After that I began to wonder how were these students able to afford all these new things. They didn't come from wealthy families so that wasn't it. I decided to ask the one who had the flat screen TV how she could afford such an expensive TV and she said "I received my refund check last week, that's how I could afford it." Even after her saying this I was still confused because the biggest refund I ever received was twenty-five dollars and I even think that was a mistake. I soon found out that students were getting hundreds, even thousands of dollars back in their refund check and instead of saving the money they were buying anything their hearts desired. What many students don't realize is that if you have student loans that refund check is not free money. It is money that will have to be paid back after graduation, so it is better to save that money for future trouble. I know that saving is one of the hardest things to do, but it is necessary if you want to survive the financial bumps in the road while in college and after!

The second semester of my freshman year was a serious financial lesson! I didn't have a cell phone because my mother could not afford the monthly payment or at least that is what she said the reason was. I had to wait for her or anyone else long distance to call me in my dorm room if we were going to talk. If I wanted to call someone I would have to buy a calling card and since the cards were expensive I was not able to get many during the semester. I only needed the calling card so that I could talk to my boyfriend who went to a college two hours away. Since I could not afford to get a calling card every week he and I would go a few days at a time without talking to each other and by the second semester of freshman year that was starting to become irritating!

One day I was sitting in the library and I overheard a group of people talking about campus codes. I didn't know what they were talking about so I sat there and eavesdropped on their entire conversation. They started to explain that these campus codes were used by non-students on campus to be able to call long distance. I thought to myself "this is the solution to my phone problem!" I didn't have the courage to ask the group what the codes were so I rushed back to the dorm to tell my roommates about what I had just heard. My roommates had not heard of the codes and it was new to them as well. We set out that day to find out what those codes were so that we could call home, since all three of us were out of state students.

Eventually one of us found a code to use and we started using it right away. I was able to make long distance phone calls without buying a calling card! I was able to talk to my boyfriend any time I wanted, for as long as I wanted! Whenever a code stopped working there was always someone on campus that knew another code that we could use. It was so bad at one point it seemed that everyone on campus had a code and was using it. We were able to use the codes almost the entire semester, but one day it all came to a halt and NONE of the codes worked anymore. Everyone including me thought that the codes were great while they lasted and now it was time to go on back to normal life with the calling cards, but SC State administrators had a different plan. Come to find out those codes did not offer free calls, but every time a code was used the university was being charged for the call! In order for the university to get their money back from the phone call charges they brought in law enforcement to find out who were the people that had the codes. It was a campus wide investigation, but the university found every person who used the codes and how much each phone call cost!

All of a sudden my roommates and I were called down to the campus police station! Can you imagine the fear that was brewing inside of me? I was so worried that they were going to kick me off the tennis team or worse kick me out of school. My worry lessened once we arrived at the police station because it appeared that the entire school was in line at the police station! When it was finally our turn we went into the office and was handed a thick stack of papers that were stapled together. My roommates and I had to sit there and go through line by line and say which calls were ours! When it was all done the financial damage was totaled. For my portion I had racked up $200 in long distance calls and it would have been more if my roommates had let me use the phone more! When we walked back to the dorm the hard part was still yet to come because we still had to tell our parents what we had done and they would have to pay the bill! I think I was so scared to call my mom that I waited until the next day. I had absolutely no money to pay the bill and neither did my roommates. My $200 bill was nothing compared to some of the other students. There were students who had bills over $1000 and the bills had to be paid because the university was threatening to send students home if they didn't pay the bill! When I called my mom and told her what happened surprisingly she didn't come down to South Carolina State and kill me, but instead said everyone makes mistakes and she paid the bill immediately. There were some students who were not as lucky and had to leave school because their parents could not pay their expensive bill!

We thought we were being creative by getting those codes for free calls, but there are actually plenty of students who are creative when it comes to making money.

Entrepreneurship: From the Dorm Room to the Board Room

Over the past few years I have met so many brilliant students from all over the world! These students are recognizing problems and coming up with ideas to solve them. They inspire me on a daily basis and I am glad that I met the following three entrepreneurs who are leaving their own mark on the world!

The first entrepreneur is **Fredrica Antwi** and she is a new entrepreneur who is gaining momentum and her company is reaching new heights each and every day! She is the founder and CEO of Locks of Curls. This entrepreneur is a current senior at the University of Maryland studying accounting and finance.

"I came up with the idea for Locks of Curls after my many trips to the beauty supply store left me broke and unhappy. I would spend so much money purchasing products but at the end of the day, they would end up in a cabinet somewhere unfinished. I wanted to come up with an exciting way for people to experiment with hair products without having to shell out too much money, and a way for people to find the products that worked for their hair. And with that, Locks of Curls was born.

Locks of Curls is still growing and things have been taking off exponentially! It's amazing how quickly your life can change when you make your hobby your job. In the past five months since I created Locks of Curls I've presented my business idea to business representatives and other successful entrepreneurs at a business pitch competition. I was blessed enough to receive a $500 grant from a Fortune 500 company which I used to pay off part of my student loan. Even though it hasn't even been half a year, I have been given so many opportunities to meet influential people and grow my business.

In the next year we plan on expanding our social media presence by uploading more YouTube videos, venturing into Instagram, and reaching out to more potential customers. We plan to launch our subscription service by January 2015 and hope that Locks of Curls continues to do well.

Website: www.locksofcurls.com

Trebreh Baaheth is a student that I met at a conference and in the midst of conversation he mentioned that he does photography. I was impressed by how he integrates his talent with his campus involvement. He has built a successful business that will truly last after graduation!

TRB Photo Designs is a full-service designing and photography business that specializes in print design and photography for any and all occasions. It was founded by Trebreh Baaheth in Baton Rouge, LA where art, designing, and pictures has been a passion of his ever since he was in elementary school. Trebreh started off drawing free handedly when he was in the fourth grade. When he joined the media department at his church is when he first saw designing digital graphics on a computer and fell in love with it. He thought it was amazing what you can do with your imagination through technology. So he immediately went into learning how to use the software: staying up all night during school nights trying to teach himself how to create his imagination. He would be up at two in the morning and would have to get up at five for school and not even be tired because he loved it just that much. "I feel like God instilled that sacrifice and drive in me to get me where I am now."

He used the talent God gave him and started TRB Photo Designs in the ninth grade. It has been a success, designing and booking photo shoots for almost seven years now for people and small businesses all over the country including some major NFL and NBA stars. He uses the money God has blessed him to make, for tithing and sowing into the kingdom, and paying off student loan debt as well as his rent and a car loan. "Although I may not pay it all off while I'm in college, I know that God will not allow me to graduate with a high debt sentence." He plans to use this amazing talent that God has given him to pay his loans in full and help his family with whatever they need. Trebreh says, "I always say never sit on the talent God has given you because it may be the very thing that will keep you out of debt and lead you into Good Success."

Trebreh Baaheth

P: (225) 303-1173

E: abohotodesigns3@gmail.com

Twitter: @toxic_foto

Facebook: facebook.com/trbphotodesigns

Instagram: @trbphotodesignz

Website: www.trbphotodesignz.co.nr

Thabiti Stephens is a young man who I heard speak at an event in Atlanta. I was in awe at Steps By Stephens mission to help fight hunger in Atlanta! This company started in a dorm room and is now a company out in the real world making a profit and making a difference! Steps by Stephens is an Atlanta based footwear company, established in 2012 by owner and CEO, Atlanta-native, Thabiti Stephens.

In 2010, nearing the end of his senior year at Atlanta's renowned Grady High School, Thabiti Stephens noticed the vast economical differences between many of his friends and classmates. Grady High School rests on the border of Atlanta's posh Midtown residences and the Boulevard community. Stephens witnessed some friends driving luxury vehicles to school at age sixteen, while others would save their lunch from school to ensure their siblings at home had food to eat. This disparity was unsettling to Stephens, and at a young age he became committed to finding ways to help improve the quality of life for the people in his city. Inspired by the philanthropic and business successes of Andrew Carnegie and John Rockefeller, Stephens was inspired to create a company that would ultimately allow him to help others.

As a long time shoe fanatic, Stephens realized what he and his friends were missing was an affordable shoe, made from high quality canvas and premium leather. Most importantly what was missing was a shoe that was not only stylish, but one that would withstand wear and tear and the pressures of time, like the impoverished families in these communities have done for generations. With this in mind, and having a natural niche for business, the day after he graduated high school, Stephens began building the infrastructure for a successful start-up company and the early designs for a timeless shoe. His desire first and foremost was to create a comfortable shoe that would help a passionate young entrepreneur improve the conditions in his community. Thus, Steps by Stephens was born.

That summer he woke every day, sat on the couch with his eyes glued to the computer. Doing research on the industry, the state of Georgia, business structure and manufacturing. Calling and emailing every manufacturer he came in contact with. By the end of that summer he had the first stages of his business plan written and the designs for which would become the signature shoe. He had yet to find a manufacturer. Going into his first semester of college he knew that he wanted to graduate with the opportunity to go work for himself. He invested every dollar that he had saved from his previous businesses, along with his graduation money. Luckily he knew a fellow freshmen who was in the start-up phases of his party promotion company. This investment helped him with thirty-five percent of his initial start-up amount. Naturally he took this opportunity to invest in him, and it paid off tremendously. At the end of that year one out of 350 manufacturers agreed to work with him. That summer Stephens worked at a fast food chain in the Atlanta airport. That money along with money from stocks he cashed, investment money and Malcolm they were ready to go. In the summer of 2012, just weeks after completing his sophomore year at Morehouse College, the first generation of Steps by Stephens's shoes was released to the world. They were made from quality canvas and leather, and available in navy blue or brown, and Steps took off around the nation.

Stephens, alongside Vice President, Malcolm Conner, promptly began presenting the Steps by Stephens's mission to friends, family, schoolmates, media personnel, and retailers. The first collection was well received by customers, the press, and most importantly the community that inspired Stephens's vision. The success in sales of the first release allowed Steps by Stephens to make impactful contributions to women and children shelters, churches, and non-profit organizations around the city of Atlanta to join in the fight against hunger.

While Stephens and Conner began preparations for the next generation of Steps, focusing on comfort and style upgrades, Steps by Stephens was featured in many local and national publications. The Steps story has been featured by Black Enterprise Magazine, Rolling Out Magazine, DC Today News, Morehouse College Maroon Tiger, and many others. Stephens has been recognized for his impressive business skills by Morehouse College and Emory University.

"At Steps by Stephens, they match style, quality and affordability unlike any other company in today's shoe industry. Effortlessly engaging the philanthropist in all of us, we invite you to join us in guilt-free shopping as you slide into your pair of Steps by Stephens.

We are looking to expand our product offering. We will increase the colors, styles and sizes that we will carry. We are looking to introduce children sizes. We are working as well as looking for retailers to carry our product. We will increase the exposure and brand awareness. Look for us to introduce a new product that follows our business model."

Website: www.stepsbystephens.com

CHAPTER SEVEN
Give Me All Your Money!

Student loan debt is a significant issue facing college students today, but it is definitely not the only one! There is something else out there that is small in its physical form, but it can take all of your money and ruin your life! It fits in the palm of your hand and can be taken anywhere in the world. Do you have an idea what I am describing yet? It is the sneaky little credit card! Credit cards have one purpose and that is to take money from you! Credit card companies have built a TRILLION dollar industry! These companies thrive on our need to have more and more stuff. They market to our "got to have it NOW!" mentality with "buy now, pay later" language that gets us to justify spending money on something we don't need! Credit card companies and their promotions are hard to avoid unless you live under a rock and I don't think anyone reading this book lives under a rock, so I am sure you experience a credit card offer at least once a day.

Credit card advertisements are everywhere! The advertisements are on TV, the radio, they come in the mail and they are even forced on you in social media! Obviously all that media was not bringing in enough money so the credit card companies searched for a new outlet and they found it in the airports. Now you can find credit card booths at large and small airports. The companies are smart too, because they only hire attractive people to work the booths. The booths are everywhere in the airport along the aisles and the way that they get your attention is to sweet talk you. I travel a lot so I get to witness their strategy firsthand and it usually goes like this:

Male employee: "Hey sweetheart, can I talk to you for a minute? This will only take a second I want to show you how awesome this airline's credit card is, and if you sign up today, today only you would get a free flight!" I bet you're thinking who would fall for that? You would be surprised to know that every airport I see those booths in that there are people lined up giving their money away! The booths obviously were not bringing in enough money so now the credit card companies are on the plane with you! I remember I was flying to Miami for a speaking engagement and I was so proud of myself because I had made it through the entire airport without being stopped by one of the people at the credit card booths. I arrived at my gate, boarded my flight, and sat down. A few minutes into the flight the flight attendant gets on the intercom and I think that she is about to give safety instructions in case the plane goes down, but instead the flight attendant starts talking about the airlines credit card and all the "benefits" the card offers. To make the advertisement complete the flight attendant said the magic phrase, "If you sign up today, today only you will receive a free flight." After that the flight attendant cut the intercom off and I thought to myself "finally I'm going to get my snack and my Coke that I just paid $200 for, but instead of the flight attendants coming down the aisle with the cart of snacks, they are walking down the aisle with credit card applications! Once again people had their hand raised begging for those applications and putting their financial lives in jeopardy. As a college student you may not have the opportunity to experience this craziness because you don't fly regularly, but there is a location that I know everyone reading this book has been in and has experienced someone offering you a credit card. That place is the clothing store! No matter what clothing store a college student walks into they will be offered a credit card! In fact the clothing store is where I fell into the credit card trap.

My third year in college I was in Minneapolis, Minnesota on my internship and I was at my favorite store at that time, The GAP, spending most of my paycheck. I finished picking out all of the clothes I wanted to buy and headed to the cashier to pay. When the cashier started ringing up the clothes she looked at me and said the universal phrase from every clothing store.

"Would you like to save twenty percent today by opening up a GAP credit card?" As she was speaking all I heard was save twenty percent and I filled out the credit card application and was approved. To show you that I didn't know what I was doing I was still trying to pay her for the clothes! She pushed my debit card back and said, "No, no, no put that away, the bill will come to you next month."

Right at that moment I knew I had made a mistake! At that moment I was on my way to becoming a statistic, because like so many other credit cardholders I forgot to pay my bill the entire month! It was not until about four days before the bill was due that I remember that I owed the money. To make the situation more urgent I was due to fly to New York the next day for a two-week business trip with my internship. This was a problem that I needed to solve quick so I rushed down to the bank and I withdrew the exact amount of money I owed GAP right down to the dimes and pennies and headed to the post office. I put all the cash in the envelope and sent it off to GAP. I went on my business trip and returned back to Minneapolis two weeks later.

When I checked my mail I was surprised to see another bill from GAP credit card services for the original amount plus a late fee! I thought right away this has to be some kind of mistake because I had paid the bill two weeks earlier. I dialed the 1-800 number and a customer service representative answered.

"Hello. Thank you for calling GAP credit card services, how may I help you?" "Hello. I am calling because there seems to be some mistake that has been made on your part. I paid a bill in full to GAP over two weeks ago, but when I looked in my mailbox today I seen a GAP bill with the amount I had already paid plus a late fee!" She replied, "I'm sorry to hear that ma'am. May I get your first and last name so that we can clear this up?" "My name is Ja'Net Mcwillis." I hear her typing on her computer on the other end of the phone. She stopped and came back to the phone. "ma'am, GAP has no records showing that you paid that bill."

By this time I am beginning to become angry because I think GAP is trying to cheat me out of my money! I took a deep breath and I told her, "I know I paid the bill because I went down to the bank and I withdrew the exact amount of money out down to the nickels and dimes. I took the money to the post office, put it in the GAP envelope and sent it to GAP!" All of a sudden I hear her quietly laughing! She then came back to the phone and said, "ma'am you're never suppose to put actual cash in an envelope. The post office probably stole your money and if they didn't I'm sure someone here at GAP did!" By this time I was angry at myself and I just hung up the phone. I went directly to my purse, took that credit card out and shredded it! Want to know what made this situation even more ridiculous is that I should not have been in it in the first place! Ever since the age of seven my mother has told me to stay away from credit cards and never get one! She use to make it a point that whenever a credit card offer came in the mail that she would walk me over to the trashcan and rip the offer up right in front of my face!

Now I know that your entire life has been filled with people telling you that you need a credit card and a credit score to participate in adulthood. They have told you that you need a credit card to rent a car, you need a credit card to book a hotel room, you need a credit score to buy a car, and you need a credit score to buy a house. Every one of those statements are false. You don't need a credit card or credit score to do any of that. I will explain later in the book how you can do each without a credit card or credit score. I know that if you knew the measures to get your credit score that you would not want to play the credit score game either. It's really simple to find what a credit score consist of on www.myfico.com. There you will find exactly what the truth behind the almighty credit score. There is a pie chart on the website that completely breaks it down. Thirty-five percent is payment history or in other words the history of us giving our money to someone else (bank, etc.), thirty percent is the amounts owed or how much money we owe other people. Fifteen percent is length of credit history and that simply means how long have we been giving money away because of debt? Ten percent is types of credit used which is how many different ways have we found to be in debt and give our money to other people, and the last ten percent is based on new credit and that is rewarding us for finding new debt to lose money on! The credit score obviously has it backwards! It is rewarding us for given our money away and not rewarding us for saving our money! That makes absolutely no sense! Credit card companies and people who say the credit score is necessary is basically saying it's okay to live your entire life in DEBT! These same people fail to mention that the average credit card debt per US adult according to data from creditcards.com is $15,480. Also that the total US outstanding revolving debt is at $870.4 BILLION and this is from TransUnion data. The Federal Reserve recent information says consumer debt is at $3.8 TRILLION. The reason that I am discussing credit cards and credit scores in a book for college students is because of the following data in 2012:

21% of college freshmen have credit card DEBT

28% of sophomores have credit card DEBT

38% of college juniors have credit card DEBT

60% of college seniors have credit card DEBT

The average student loan debt that the most recent graduating class had was $33,000, so why should anyone encourage college students to get a credit card that more than likely will add thousands of dollars to the debt they already have?

If you decide after reading this chapter that you will never have a credit card again and you won't worry about a credit score know that people will look at you like you have a third eye. People who use credit card debt to live will not understand why you won't become a part of their revolving nightmare! They will attempt to bring you back on board by saying, "it's okay to have a credit card as long as you pay it off every month." These people don't take this phrase seriously "what can happen, usually will!" Something could happen and you use the credit card to pay for it and end up in debt for a long time! Another favorite of credit card fans is the famous credit card points for "free stuff!" There is data (Dunn & Bradstreet) that says people with credit cards spend twelve to eighteen percent more money and these credit card reward points feed right into that mentality. The problem with credit card reward points is that you spend more money to get the reward you'd have if you would have just bought the reward right out. I know of a credit card that gives a penny for every dollar spent, so imagine how much you have to spend to get the free flight that's worth 25,000 or more points! It's better to just buy the flight with your own money and tell the credit card company, "no thank you!"

CHAPTER EIGHT
What Are You Waiting For?

No matter what year you are in college whether you are at a two-year or a four-year institution you have to start today! Today is the day you make it up in your mind that you are not going to struggle financially anymore. You are no longer going to have money on Monday and by Saturday your pockets are empty and you're wondering where it all went. From this day forth you will know how much money is coming in and how much money is going out every month. Today your money no longer controls you, you control it! So how do you get to this point?

Let's start with freshmen, sophomores, and those at a two year institutions looking to finish at a four year institution who are at the beginning of their college and financial journey. As freshmen you are the new people on campus so it is your time to hustle so that you can start your college career off right! See if you hustle and work hard it will always pay off. I am sure you are saying to yourself "of course if people work hard they will be successful!", but if that's true why doesn't everyone do it? Why doesn't everyone work hard? I tell you what, I didn't always work hard, but I know why I didn't work hard. Well at least I convinced other people that I didn't work hard. See when I was in high school I don't know why, but I didn't want people to know I got good grades. For some reason the thought of people actually thinking that I was smart really embarrassed me. I thought it was cool for people to think I was dumb. The teacher would ask a question and even if I knew the answer you were not going to catch me with my hand in the air like I was when Hank was giving out those fifty dollar bills. No... way! In fact whenever I would get my exams back I would hurry up and stuff them in my book bag so no one would see the "A". There was one person I didn't mind seeing my grades and that was my mother. From time to time she would ask me "So how did you do on your algebra test?" I proudly took my crumbled up test out of my book bag and showed her my "A". My mother is a smart woman and after a while she started to catch on and she asked me "why are all your papers always crumbled up?" I looked at her and when an answer would not come out I realized that I honestly did not know what to say!

That's when I figured it out that the thing that really embarrassed me the most was standing out from the crowd in any way. So I wasn't embarrassed by the good grades I really was just embarrassed whenever I was different from the people I was around. This behavior continued to my actual graduation day from college! I remember walking across the stage at my college graduation and after my name the announcer saying Summa Cum Laude and I went back to my seat and sat down. All of a sudden this guy by the name of Raymond turned around to me and before I go on, you have to understand that Raymond was a cutie.

If you are a guy reading this book you may want to skip down a few lines while I describe Raymond to the women reading this book. Raymond was fine! He was one of the most popular guys on campus. I'm not saying that I liked him because I had a boyfriend at the time, all I am saying is that all the girls on campus loved them some Raymond. Once I sat down Raymond looked confusingly at the stage, then he looked at me, then back at the stage, then back to me and said "Ja'Net you're Summa Cum Laude? Man if I'd known that I would have been cheating off of you a long time ago." As he was talking to me in my mind I was saying "Go Ja'Net it's your birthday" but on my face I just had a slight smile and said confidently "yeah Raymond I've been getting good grades this whole time."

It was interesting the thing that I feared the most getting good grades, standing out was the thing that caused me to be selected for one of the biggest opportunities of my life. That internship I was talking about with one of the top companies in the world! See because I took care of business in the classroom, and because I stood out academically it was a paid internship. An internship that people would die to get. Some people spend a part of their adult life trying to get a sales job with this company. Don't be ashamed to do your best each and every day! I wasted four years hiding from success and I would not recommend that for anyone!

College is also a time where you can explore many different things. There are many clubs and organizations that are on campus and they will help you develop character. Some organizations help with professionalism, networking, leadership, and it would be in your best interest to find one that fits you. It is extremely important to get involved on campus because internships during undergrad and jobs after graduation are going to hire people who were active outside of the classroom!

Grades and campus involvement are vital for your resume no matter what year you are in college. Freshmen need to start researching "PAID" internships. As a freshman you may not get an internship the first summer, but you may get some interviewing practice in with a company recruiter. By doing this you will be more prepared than everyone else that decided to wait until sophomore year to start interviewing. If you are not able to get an internship at the end of your freshman year it doesn't mean you just sit around all summer watching TV. Look for a job where you live at so that you can be making money throughout the summer. All the money you make over the summer is for a purpose. A lot a people whether they are in college or not, spend every dollar they get and so it makes it hard for them to become debt free. When you spend all your money on your wants you won't have the money when it is time to take care of your needs! When you start getting paid you have to find the discipline to save as much money as possible. The money that you save can be used for any emergencies during your sophomore year.

Take for example a scholarship that you won was not the original amount stated and it is not enough money to cover tuition for the semester. You end up owing the school money before they will let you go to class. The extra money you earn can be used to cover that! The money you make on your summer job is also for years from now. If you have student loan debt, when you graduate from college you will have money saved to start paying it off!

Sophomores it is more important to land an internship in the summer. During the summer after sophomore year a student should start testing the waters of certain industries to see if it is an area they would like to work in after college. When sophomores make the decision about the industry they want to work in they can move towards researching the different companies within that industry and which companies are thriving and which companies are just surviving.

Sophomores need to also see which one of those companies offer "paid" internships so that they can send in an application immediately! The goal is to get an internship at the company that you want to work for in the future. This is the type of approach that I took when looking for that internship I mentioned earlier. It was hard for me to find the time for an internship, but if you don't have the same constraints that I had, it is in your best interest to get a "paid" internship. I am sure by now you have noticed the word "paid" when I mention internships. The first reason that I want students to go after "paid" internships is of course to get money to pay off debt. The other less obvious reason that students should search for "paid" internships is that I feel that if you are working for someone and making their company money then you should be compensated for that! What if the internship is in a city that you have to move to? Then they should pay you so that you are able to afford to live in another city. Last, but not least if you do an "unpaid", internship, what is the odds that the company is going to give you a reasonable salary after graduation? The way they see it you worked for free in the past, why do they need to pay you the industry average or higher. When you take an unpaid internship 99.9% of the time you are cheating yourself.

Now for the juniors, seniors, and those going for a two year degree only life is a little more serious because the clock is ticking, and in the blink of an eye you will be walking across the graduation stage into the real world! Juniors who have student loans should take the time during this year to find out what is the balance of their student loans. Yes, they have one more year of cost to think about, but it is better to get an idea of the amount of debt you have before senior year. By your junior year you should have worked at least one internship and if not, have worked for two consecutive summers. If you have not done so already take the money that you made from the internships and jobs and put it in a savings account. The main reason that it needs to go into savings and not checking is because the money needs to be in a place not easily accessible to you. If it is in checking your friends could come up to you one Friday and convince you to go on a weekend road trip and since the money is easy to get out because it is in checking, you withdraw it and hit the road! Then on Monday you feel bad because you spent your hard earned money. Junior year is a great time for you to ramp up your bank account. In the past you may have only worked during the summer, but during your junior year try to work during Christmas and spring break.

You will need to make as much money as you can so that you can have enough to get a head start on paying off debt after graduation. Even if you don't have debt you can still make money to put into your emergency fund! The goal is to have as much money possible saved after graduation so that you don't struggle to live on your own.

I did not follow this advice of saving as much as I could from my internship and other jobs and it cost me thousands! I lost the most money during the internship in Minneapolis, Minnesota. Everything had the opportunity to take money out of my pocket and I never even put up a fight. Music concerts talked me out of my money, vacations and expensive dinners told me it was okay to give them my money, even someone I don't even know personally got money out of me. Shawn Carter or you may know him by his celebrity name Jay-Z is the one who almost took the largest sum of money from me.

So I was on the internship during the summer after my junior year and at that time I had to major loves that controlled my life. My first love is the same love that a lot of women have and that is shoes! I remember that summer being infatuated with these pair of boots! All the stars were wearing these boots on television. Beyonce was sporting them, Eve and JLo had a pair and I thought to myself "if these millionaires have a pair then obviously I Ja'Net the BROKE college student should have a pair too! Unfortunately there was a major problem and that problem was that I did not know the name of the boots. Now my second love during that time was music, especially Hip Hop. My favorite rapper back then was Jay-Z and I knew every word to every song Jay-Z ever had! One night I was sitting in my apartment in Minneapolis looking at music videos on MTV when Jay-Z's hit song with his now wife Beyoncé "Bonnie and Clyde" came on.

I was sitting alone in my apartment so the only logical next step was to stand up and start acting out the music video! I started by rapping all of Jay-Z's parts, then I would switch over and start singing Beyoncé's part and I went back and forth until Jay-Z said the words that made my heart skip a beat! Jay-Z said the magical words Manolo Blahnik Timbs and voila` there were THE BOOTS on the screen! These boots were perfect, because they looked like Timberland boots, but they had six inch heels on them which made it perfect for women! When I finally seen the shoes I think I started hyperventilating because I couldn't believe that the moment had come where the name of my dream boots were no longer a mystery! Immediately I ran to the bedroom where the computer was, all the while repeating Manolo Blahnik, Manolo Blahnik, Manolo Blahnik! I sat down at the computer and opened up Google to search for it. It actually took me thirty minutes just to spell Manolo Blahnik correctly, but when I found the shoes at the New York store, ooh wee those shoes were $700! $700 for some shoes! Now remember I am making $3K a month on this internship so I can afford to buy these shoes, but I could not fathom the thought of spending that amount of money on something that would go on my feet! For something that I would be walking on concrete with! So what was my next option?

Well, about a couple of months later Steve Madden came out with its own version of Manolo Blahnik Timbs. I remember being back in that same bedroom on that same computer searching the Steve Madden website. As I was waiting I was praying to myself please don't let these shoes cost more than rent! Guess what? They didn't cost $700, the Steve Madden version only cost eighty dollars! The Steve Madden pair looked EXACTLY the same and cost $620 less! I said to myself now that's more like it and I ordered the shoes right away. The boots were on back order so that gave me some time to finish the internship, go back to South Carolina State the next semester and wait patiently on my shoes! I waited so patiently that every day in between classes I would call my mom. On Monday I asked her "have my shoes arrived yet?" On Tuesday "mama have you seen my shoes?" I skipped Wednesday because I didn't want to look desperate, but on Thursday "mama please make sure they don't steal my boots off the porch!" The waiting was getting so bad that I called UPS with my tracking number making sure they didn't lose my boots! I bet you are thinking "why in the world is she going so crazy over some boots?" It's because at the time Steve Madden didn't have a presence in the south where South

Carolina State was. There were no stores so I was guaranteed to be the first one on campus with these boots!

Now when it comes to spending money to impress other people you tend to bring someone else into that madness and that someone else for me was my mother. Once the shoes arrived at the house FINALLY, I actually convinced her to bring the shoes three hours down the road to where I was at South Carolina State and being the angel that she is she did it. Thanks to my mother I was the first one on campus to have the shoes and I must admit I was the "IT" girl for like a whole month!

I promise I wore those boots every day of that month. I wore the shortest skirts and the shortest shorts so everyone could see my boots. I didn't even care if it was cold outside, I would just put on a pair of tights and kept it moving! You should have seen me walking through campus with my new boots! I would walk past the dorms and the people standing outside would whisper "ooh ahh, look Ja'Net got the new Manolo's." I would go to the cafeteria and walk to the line to get my food and I would hear the girls whispering to one another as I walked by. One girl would whisper "oooh ahhhh how did Ja'Net afford the Manolo's?" Her friend would respond, "you didn't know she was on that internship last semester that must be how she could afford them!" I loved the attention so it was no way that I was going to correct them! Unfortunately the attention only lasted for a month because somehow everyone else found out about Steve Madden. I started seeing different colors and styles of the boots and just like that I was no longer the "IT" girl. When I looked back on the situation I jumped through all those hoops for a pair of boots, and I did it all just to impress other people! When everyone else had the boots it showed me that all those ooh ahhh people never really cared about me, all they cared about were those boots!

Do other people cause you to spend money? If you see someone with the hottest new brand of clothing does it make you want to go out and buy it so that everyone will say ooh ahhh to you? If you spend money to impress other people while in college it won't stop when you graduate it will only continue. There are people in their sixties still buying brand new cars because they want to impress people at their job! Trying to impress people may only cost you a couple of hundred dollars in college, but if you continue with that mindset after college it will cost you tens of thousands of dollars! The career that you will go into after college is going to pay you the most money you have ever made and you need to be prepared to handle it!

Hopefully by your junior year you have an idea of the industry that you want to work in, and maybe even the company that you want to work for. In order to get hired in today's world you have to be more creative. Sending out hundreds of resumes is not enough anymore to land you that dream career. You have to search deeper for the "hidden" jobs and that takes creativity and perseverance! It takes getting up from the computer and going out and networking with people, because it is people that have the inside information on available jobs. It is people that will get your resume to the right person instead of it getting rejected by a computer system.

Become a familiar face at the career center on campus and let each person in the center know what you are looking for. The professionals in the career center have long standing relationships with companies and they may know someone who could point you in the right direction for that job you want after graduation. Also when you are home during breaks or the summer after your junior year make sure to connect with friends of your parents. Let them know what you are pursuing career wise so they can be looking for it within the companies they work for and if it is nothing where they work at, they may know someone at another company and put in a good word for you! Your parents should be working on your behalf as well. They should let their friends and associates know that you will be graduating in a year and what you are looking to do career wise.

Another idea is to start following companies on social media. If a company is forward thinking they are all over social media. On social media they will post events and news stories that will help you research the company on a deeper level. Through social media you can find people who work for the company and connect with them. Through that connection you may even be able to set up an informational interview with that person and discuss their insights about the company. All of this is to help you during the interview process. Who do you think the company will hire?

The person who just came in talking about themselves and how great they are or the person who comes in and knows that the company plans to open up a branch in Shanghai because they are trying to conquer the Asian market before their competition. The company will hire the person who has done their research because they see that if the person did that much work just for the interview imagine how hard they will work once they are inside the corporation!

Lastly, the seniors who have the least amount of time before graduation. I don't know how many times I have talked to a senior after a speaking engagement who said they did not know what they were going to do after graduation! They didn't know where they were going to work, if they were going back to school, nothing! If you have debt and you say "I don't know what I'm doing after graduation," you are basically saying "I don't know how I am going to pay off this debt!" Not knowing what you are going to do about paying off debt after graduation will guarantee that you will be harassed by the people you owe the money to! The student loan companies love to call you every day all day! They will email you and contact your parents! Why do they go through all of this? Because they want their money! Student loans are not like other debt, because it cannot be discharged in bankruptcy. Mortgages, credit card debt, medical debt, can be discharged in bankruptcy, but student loans are nearly impossible to get rid of without paying them off! There has been a case where a woman with student loans was on disability and could not work, but she could not get rid of the student loans in bankruptcy. If you have government backed loans the government WILL get their money one way or another!

If you have a job the government can garnish your wages, which means they can take up to fifteen percent of your disposable income. Imagine that your budget is tight and you make just enough money $1000 or so, to cover all of your expenses and all of a sudden your paycheck is cut by $150 (fifteen percent) to $850. Now you don't have enough money to pay all of your bills so you start to go into more debt. To make the numbers work you start using credit cards and digging yourself a deeper hole! The government can also take your income tax refund every year that you do not pay your student loan. They can take the refund until your student loan is paid off.

The government can sue you for non-payment on the student loan and unlike other debts there isn't a time limit on how long they can go after you. They can sue you forever! The government can also take a portion of your social security check once you turn sixty-five. It can take up to fifteen percent out as long as they leave you $750 a month! There are people who went back to college in their fifties and racked up student loan debt. Now that they are in retirement and need the entire social security check they are finding that their money is being taken because they have unpaid student loans! If you pass away and still have student loans the federal loans may be forgiven, but private student loans are completely different and more than likely will have to be paid out of your estate. All of these situations are a headache so it is best to just pay the student loans off!

At the beginning of your senior year you have to put yourself in the best position possible for a good job after graduation. You need a decent salary if you are going to be able to live on your own and pay off debt! If you have $50,000 in student loan debt you cannot come out making $25,000 a year because it is going to take you a long time to pay the debt off. Try your best to make sure the income is higher than the debt you owe because that will allow you to become debt free quicker. There are steps that you can take before graduation to ensure financial success after college.

Your GPA is the first step. The two semesters of your senior year can be used to get the best grades possible in the classes you have left. You don't have to be the top of your graduating class, but you definitely don't want to be mediocre or below average. Some companies won't even look at your resume if you don't have a certain GPA. It's not fair, but it is their rules and job candidates have to abide by them. There are different ways that you can raise your GPA. One being you can study day and night to make sure you have everything memorized for upcoming tests. Another option is to become best friends with your professors. You don't have to hang out with them or anything, but at least show genuine interest in the class and what they are teaching you. This technique actually worked for me!

There was this class with this professor who shall remain nameless, but everyone hated this class and was afraid of this professor because he gave out "F's" like they were lollipops! The bad part about the class is that if you were a business major you needed the class to graduate so this professor had power over every student in the business school! The class was so difficult to pass that some people begged for permission from the dean to take the class at a different institution during the summer.

I needed an "A" out of this class in order to obtain Summa Cum Laude status and after all of the horror stories from students who had taken the class I knew I had to try a different approach. I decided to go to class on the first day, sit down close to the front, and listen to every word he said so that I could pick up on something that would give me an advantage. It was not until the middle of the three hour class that he said if you want to get ahead in this class you need to listen to NPR. There it was! The key to me getting my "A", but there was one problem I didn't know what NPR stood for! I decided to raise my hand and ask him what NPR was. He let me, as well as everyone else in the class know that NPR stood for National Public Radio and it was basically talk radio that showcased programs that covered domestic and world events. He told us that if we listened to NPR that it would benefit us greatly because each week he would ask us questions from the programs. His strategy was genius because the class only met once a week so if we wanted to know the answers to the questions he was going to ask we would have to listen to NPR all week!

If he wanted me to listen to every program on NPR in order to get that "A", then listen I was going to do! Every time I was in the car I was listening to NPR. My friends would ride with me and complain constantly about wanting to listen to music. They absolutely hated listening to a station that only had news on it with no commercials! Even though I was making my friends miserable I knew that I had to do whatever it took to make a positive impression in that class! It got so bad that at one point I was taking notes on the news programs so that I could review them before going to class. The professor stayed true to his word and when we met on that Monday and every Monday after during that semester he asked questions from the NPR shows. Every class that semester I made sure my hand was up to answer every question!

NPR was the first key to success in this class, but the second key was to make sure that the professor knew who I was and that I was interested in his class. In order to show that interest I went to his office from time to time to ask questions about different class assignments and projects. At first I was doing it so that he could put a face with a name, but as time went on I found out that he was actually willing to help me with anything that I did not understand. That help allowed me to change course on a particular class assignment leading to a higher grade on that assignment. At the end of the semester right before graduation I received my "A" and was able to walk across the stage with Summa Cum Laude status! I learned a lot from this situation about myself and about others. All of those students who had horror stories about the class obviously thought that it would be like other classes where you just show up and hope to get an "A". That you would not need to do anything extra other than take tests and complete projects. This class was far from that because the professor wanted to know that the students cared and were invested in the material. That is why he had the NPR component as part of the class because he wanted to create a separation in the class. He wanted to separate the students with initiative from the students who were just trying to get by with a passing grade.

The NPR requirement was really simple because you only had to listen to a radio station, but I was surprised every week at the people who never raised their hands because they had not listened to the radio station! This professor taught me that nothing is going to just be given to you! You are going to have to take initiative and go for what you want! I am thankful to that professor for introducing me to NPR because I still listen to it today and because NPR keeps me informed of domestic and international news I have been able to stay ahead of my business competition!

Your GPA is just the beginning, next you need to start putting together a list of all the extracurricular activities that you have been involved with during your college career. These activities will show a potential employer that you are a well-rounded person. Extracurricular activities can show that you are a leader, creative, team player, ambitious, outgoing, and any of these traits may give you an advantage over another person who is interviewing for the same job! Companies need to see that you didn't go back and forward between class and your room, but that you went out and interacted with others. Interaction is key because every day in your career you will be interacting with others to solve problems! Make sure to list community activities as well as what you were involved with during breaks from school. Companies usually have a philanthropic and volunteering division within and would love to see that the person that they are interviewing has an interest in reaching out to the community.

Now that you have the grades and extracurricular activities in place now it is time to go out and connect with potential employees who can help you from the inside. With the juniors I talked about reaching out on social media and following companies, but as a senior you have to take it up a notch! You need to connect with alumni through social media. Not just any alumni, but look for those alumni who are employed at the companies you are targeting. Make an honest effort to reach out to them and let them know that you are interested in learning more about the company and if they would be willing to share their insights. You can even take it a step further and ask if they would be available to talk by phone to answer any questions you have. You want to do all of this so that you can build a relationship with the alum that is in the company. Alumni want to help students from their alma mater, but they also want to make sure you are a fit for the job because it is their reputation on the line. Informational telephone calls will help them determine if you are worth them bringing your name up to human resources. Another connection that you must consider are your professors. I know that the last thing on your mind is to spend any more time than you have to with your professors, but they may be able to help you land a job after college. You have to realize that some of your professors have been at the institutions for years, maybe even a decade or more so they know a lot of former students. These former students will keep in contact with their favorite professors and may even call them to ask if they know of any students that would be a fit for a job at their company. You want to be that student that the professor mentions so make sure as soon as you start your senior year go to a few of your professors and ask them about their alumni contacts!

Getting that salary secured may seem like the hard part, but it is what you do with that salary after graduation that is the true test! The decisions that a recent graduate makes in the first few months are the decisions that can make or break their financial future. This is what usually happens after graduation that keeps someone in debt for the rest of their lives. A person graduates from college and starts working at their new job. At this new job they are earning the most money they have ever earned in their life and immediately start to think of ways to spend it! The problem with this plan is that a lot of graduates have student loan debt, in fact the most recent data states that seven out of ten graduates left with debt! There is a six month grace period before you have to start paying your student loans monthly and it is during that six month period that bad decisions are made. The recent college graduate looks at the amount of money in their paycheck and thinks to themselves I need an apartment, but not just any apartment will do. They go and sign the lease to a two bedroom luxury apartment with the exercise room and pool!

They have the new apartment and realize they need furniture so the next stop is the "buy now, pay later!" furniture store. Since these stores make it simple for the buyer by selling entire rooms for one price it is very easy to buy $4000 worth of furniture on credit and think that you will pay it off later. Once the person has the apartment and the furniture inside it is time to get a new car with a car payment so that they can drive back and forward from their home and job. Now that they have a new apartment and car payment it is obviously time to go on vacation, and not just any vacation, but the vacation is probably to an island! So in the six months leading up to the start of student loan repayment the person has apartment rent which could cost them $1000 or more depending on where they live and a car payment which could be $300 or more a month! The car also comes with other expenses like car insurance, gas, and repairs which will take more money out of their monthly paycheck! In a short period of time after graduation the person has managed to assign more than $1500 or more to paying bills and that is before they buy food!

At this point is where their financial life starts to go downhill! Because of all the new expenses their spending plan or budget is completely stretched, so when the student loan bill comes six months after graduation they don't have the money to pay it and still pay other bills. This leads to deferment or forbearance of the student loan which could lead in some cases the interest accruing during the time that the person is not paying the monthly payment. Now they are only going deeper in debt every month because the student loan balance continues to grow!

If you are reading this book and you don't have student loans don't think that you are in the clear and that your finances are going to work out great, because I was you and I still ended up in $48,000 of debt! I graduated from college debt free and immediately started spending my paycheck. I didn't rent the two bedroom luxury apartment, but I rented a house! I went to the furniture store and bought $6000 of furniture on a "buy now, pay later" plan and with any money I had left I went shopping every week! Even if you don't have debt you can still be irresponsible with money that can lead you into having debt in the future.

CHAPTER NINE
It's Up To YOU!

I can give you all the tips to win with money and live your dreams, but unless you make it up in your mind to do it, it won't work! The "make your mind up and do it mentality" works with every part of your life, not just your money. When you make up your mind to stand out from the crowd you will win with money and you will win at life! Stand out students get the paid internships that lead to high salary jobs that provide you the money to pay off debt! Professors are looking for students who stand out, employers are looking for job candidates who stand out, and the world is looking for people who stand out because it is those people who can change the world! If you decide not to stand out, then you are making the decision to miss out on opportunities that can advance your finances. On "the Wednesday" I decided not to stand out and it cost me $300 from Hank Allan. I made a mistake that day and I knew it! Throughout the rest of your life you will make mistakes, you will fall down, but it is how you recover from the mistakes and failures that will determine if you are successful or not.

After I missed out on the money from Hank I made my mind up that I would never be in that situation again and I would always stand out. A couple of days after "the Wednesday" I was sitting on the fourth floor of the business building feeling sorry for myself because I had failed to do my best in front of Hank. I remember someone talking to me as I looked out the window into the parking lot. After five minutes of gazing depressingly out the window I saw a car pull into the parking lot and drive towards the business building. Inside the car was a familiar face, Mr. Hank Allan driving towards where I was at! Immediately the depression was gone and I had jumped out of my chair, gathered my papers, so I could run down the steps to meet Hank. I ran down four flights of steps at full speed so that I could meet him before he walked into the building. I finally arrived at the bottom and made it to the entrance, but before I walked outside I had to stop panting and catch my breath. I finally caught my breath, opened the door and walked casually towards Hank. As I neared him I faked tripped and dropped all of my papers in front of him so that he would stop and help me pick them up. As he was helping me pick up everything I looked at him and said, "you're Hank Allan right?"

He replied, "Yes, I'm Hank Allan."

Then I continued, "You're the one that was giving out fifty dollar bills the other day for answers about the Orangeburg Massacre! I knew all the answers and you never called on me!" I looked down at his pockets "do you have $50 now? Ask me a question I bet you I know the answer!" Hank started to laugh and I laughed as well, but then I stopped and became serious and asked him, "Mr. Allan what do I need to do to be successful?"

Hank replied, "Well you've already taken the first step, you're in college, what are your grades like?" You know how I use to be ashamed for people to know that I got good grades? I was not ashamed that day! I told him I had made straight A's the previous semester. Hank went on "Okay, you have the first step, now the second step to being successful is are you involved on campus? Do you participate in anything outside of the classroom?" Enthusiastically I replied "YES! I am on the tennis team and I am a member of Alpha Kappa Psi business fraternity!" A surprised look came upon his face and he said, "Ja'Net, you play tennis? My son plays tennis and I have been trying to find ways to connect with him more through tennis. Do you have any recommendations?" I gave him a few phone numbers of tennis professionals in the city where he lived and a couple other pieces of advice that could help his son and him connect more.

Hank thanked me and we parted ways for then, but you know that internship that I was talking about earlier? Well, it was given to me by Hank Allan himself at Pfizer Pharmaceuticals! Yes, I missed out on $300 on "the Wednesday", but Hank added a "0" to the end of it and made it a $3000 a month paycheck!

STAND OUT!

CHAPTER TEN
HOW TO:

1. Rent A Car Without A Credit Card

2. Book A Hotel Room Without A Credit Card

3. Buy A Car Without A Credit Score

4. Buy A House Without A Credit Score

5. Rent An Apartment Without A Credit Score

6. Do Your Dream Sheet

7. Do Your Spending Plan

Rent A Car Without A Credit Card

I travel a lot and since I do not own a credit card the only way that I am able to rent a car is through the use of my debit card. I have rented from all the top car rental companies and have never encountered a problem. Understand that you will have some extra steps when using a debit card, but I find that I am through the line and in the rental car just as quickly as the person with the credit card!

The most important information that you need to know about renting a car with a debit card is that the car rental company is going to put a "hold" on your bank account. A "hold" is where the company will tie up a certain amount of money in your account while you have the car in your possession. This "hold" usually ranges between $200-$500, but I have never seen a "hold" more than $300. This amount is in addition to the rental car rate. At this point some people say, "I can't afford for them to freeze $200 in my bank account. In fact I may not even have $200 in my bank account!" If you can't afford a hold

on your account from a car rental company then maybe

you should not be spending money on a rental car. If you

decide to go and rent a car make sure you let the company

know up front that you will be using a debit card so that

they will let you know what is required.

Book A Hotel Room Without A Credit Card

Booking a hotel room with a debit card is a lot like

the car rental process. The hotel will put a "hold" on your

account in addition to the cost of the hotel room. The hotel

takes this action to have insurance against you in case you

decide to lose your mind temporarily and trash their room!

You can use your debit card online to book with any hotel

or travel website and usually the website will allow you to

cancel anytime before day of arrival and not charge your

bank account. Booking a hotel is another situation that if

you can't afford for them to put a hold on your account

then you should skip staying at a hotel. For those of you

who can afford the hold when you arrive at the hotel make

sure that you have your debit card as well as a valid I.D. so that check-in will go smoothly!

Buy A Car Without A Credit Score

Before I started to write this book I went on social media and asked my community of college students what type of financial questions would they want answered. This question was asked by Christopher Thomas and he wanted to know how to buy a car without a credit score. I told Christopher that I would make sure to answer the question in the book so here it is!

The reason that a car dealership needs to check your credit score is because you are borrowing money. So what happens when you don't borrow money? That's right! A credit score doesn't matter! When I am at a speaking event this is usually the time when a student raises their hand and says, "how am I going to buy a new car with cash?" Then I have to explain that they are not buying a new car with cash, but that they are going to save their money and buy a used car. I go on to show them how they will pay themselves a car payment ($100, $200, $300) each month for a year or two and buy a used car with cash! If a student pays themselves $300 a month for a year they will have $3600 and that is more than enough to get you a reliable used car. Students should also look into car and police auctions for inexpensive used cars. If you can find a police auction those are usually the best because the police do not own the car and will sell it for a lower price!

Buy A House Without A Credit Score

College students have only known what most Americans know and that is after college a person who wants to eventually own a home must have a high credit score to qualify for a loan. What about those of us that do not want to play the "go into debt in order to get a high credit score game?" There is another way, but before I explain how, know that if you go get a mortgage your credit score needs to be 650 and higher or at zero. You can't have a credit score in the 400s and think that a bank is going to give you a mortgage. If I go get a mortgage with a zero credit score then I will need extra documentation.

First I will need twelve to twenty four months of on time monthly rent payments. This shows that I am responsible and I won't miss a mortgage payment. Other documents in addition to the rent payments that can help you qualify for a mortgage are phone bills, cable bills, renter, and car insurance payments. You must show the lender that you pay everything on time and can be trusted. All of these documents are great, but there is something that will get you closer to a mortgage approval and that is a substantial down payment. It is best to have a down payment of twenty percent or more because this means that you are truly serious about the property you want to buy. As you can see I just provided you with a way to get a mortgage without falling into the credit trap!

Rent An Apartment Without A Credit Score

I never rented an apartment while in college and I was still able to rent an apartment right after graduation. I didn't go to an apartment complex where the company checks credit scores, but instead I researched people who owned rental properties. Individuals who own their own rental property will overlook someone with a zero credit score because all they care about is if you can pay your rent to them every month! I was able to show the owner that I had a job and that my income would definitely cover the rent and utilities. Once the rental property owner seen the documentation the property was mine. The first property that I rented was a two story house with a garage and a backyard. The second property I rented was a three level town home with a garage and both of these properties had rents that were less than a two bedroom apartment! Before graduation start researching rental properties in the area that you will be living, budget for the rent, and you will be able to get a great property for a low cost with no credit check!

DREAM SHEET

SHORT TERM: 3-6 MONTHS

1. _____

2. _____

3. _____

INTERMEDIATE: 1-2 YEARS

1. _____

2. _____

3 _____

LONG TERM: 3-5 YEARS

1. _____

2. _____

3. _____

SPENDING PLAN

Income

Paycheck	0
Financial Aid	0
Money From Parents	0
Money Gifts	0
Other	0

Expenses

Giving	0
Saving	0
Cell Phone	0
Clothing	0
Car Payment	0
Car Insurance	0
Car Repairs	0
Rent	0
Cable	0
Energy Bill	0
Water Bill	0
Tuition	0
Books	0
Supplies	0
Parking	0
Internet	0
Gas	0
Entertainment	0
Groceries	0
Dining Out	0

SPENDING PLAN (continued)

Expenses (continued)

Clothing	0
Hair	0
Student Loan Payment	0
Organization Fees	0
Renters Insurance	0
Credit Card Payoff	0
Other	0
Other	0
Other	0
Income-Expenses=	0

JA'NET ADAMS is an international speaker and author who helps college students realize their dreams! She is one of the top financial literacy speakers in the country and through her engaging keynotes and workshops she helps college students think differently about their finances! After helping thousands of students get a handle on their money so they can pursue their dreams she was given the nickname "Dream Girl"! The college student who gave her the nickname said, "because you have shown me how to control my money I will be able to pursue my dream of starting a non profit that helps children go to college!" Ja'Net's advice has been featured in USA Today College, BBC.com, CNBC.com, Black Business Ink, Campus Programming Magazine, College Smart Radio, and so much more! Ja'Net says "I think that every college student has a dream that can change the world and I want to make sure debt doesn't keep them from making those dreams a reality!

Dr. Wallace,

It was nice to
meet you! I
hope you enjoy
the book!

Brian

Dr. Wallace,

It was nice to meet you! I hope you enjoy the book!

[signature]

Made in the USA
San Bernardino, CA
29 March 2016